D1531074

Rhinoceroses and Hippopotamuses

Michael and Jane Pelusey

Marshall Cavendish
Benchmark
New York

Marshall Cavendish Benchmark
99 White Plains Road
Tarrytown, NY 10591
www.marshallcavendish.us

First published in 2008 by
MACMILLAN EDUCATION AUSTRALIA PTY LTD
15–19 Claremont Street, South Yarra 3141

Visit our Web site at www.macmillan.com.au or go directly to www.macmillanlibrary.com.au

Associated companies and representatives throughout the world.

Library of Congress Cataloging-in-Publication Data

Pelusey, Michael.
   Rhinoceroses and hippopotamuses / by Michael and Jane Pelusey.
   p. cm. — (Zoo animals)
   Includes index.
   ISBN 978-0-7614-3150-3
   1. Rhinoceroses—Juvenile literature. 2. Hippopotamidae—Juvenile
literature. 3. Zoo animals—Juvenile literature. I. Pelusey, Jane. II.
Title.
   SF408.6.R45P45 2008
   636.9668—dc22

                                                        2008001660

Edited by Margaret Maher
Text and cover design by Christine Deering
Page layout by Christine Deering
Illustrations by Gaston Vanzet

Printed in the United States

Acknowledgments
Michael and Jane Pelusey would like to thank Perth Zoo, Melbourne Zoo, Werribee Wildlife Zoo; and Taronga Zoo for their assistance during this project.

Cover photograph: White rhinoceros at a wildlife zoo, courtesy of Pelusey Photography.

All photographs © Pelusey Photography except for Global Gypsies, 10, 11, 20, 30;
Shutterstock/Jiri Cvrk, 19.

1   3   5   6   4   2

Contents

Glossary words
When a word is printed in **bold**, you can look up its meaning in the Glossary on page 31.

Zoos

Zoos are places where animals that are usually **wild** are kept in **enclosures**. Some zoos have a lot of space for animals to move about. They are called wildlife zoos.

Different kinds of animals sometimes live in one large enclosure at a wildlife zoo.

Zoo Animals

Zoos keep all kinds of animals. People go to zoos to learn about animals. Some animals may become **extinct** if left to live in the wild.

Some people visit zoos to learn about animals they have never seen before.

Rhinoceroses and Hippopotamuses

Rhinoceroses are very big with tough wrinkly skin. They have one or two horns at the front of their heads. There are five different kinds of rhinoceroses.

horn

wrinkly skin

The white rhinoceros is one of the biggest kinds of rhinoceros.

Hippopotamuses are also big animals, but they are smaller than rhinoceroses. Hippopotamuses spend some of their time in water. There are two different kinds of hippopotamuses.

The common hippopotamus is the bigger hippopotamus.

The rare pygmy hippopotamus is the smaller hippopotamus.

In the Wild

In the wild, rhinoceroses live in Asia and Africa. Most rhinoceroses live in woodlands, but white rhinoceroses are found on open grasslands.

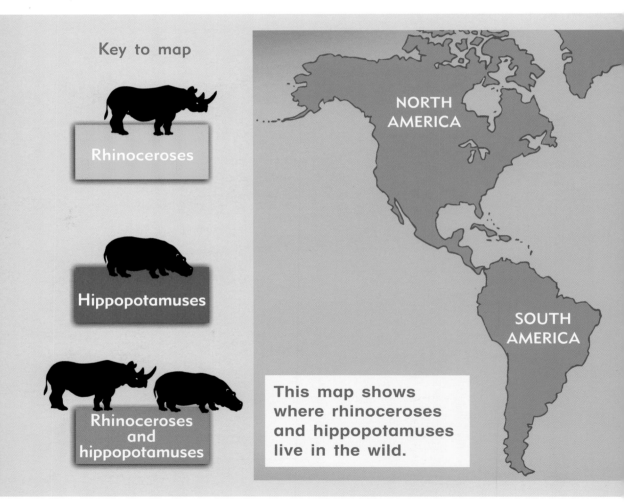

Key to map

Rhinoceroses

Hippopotamuses

Rhinoceroses and hippopotamuses

NORTH AMERICA

SOUTH AMERICA

This map shows where rhinoceroses and hippopotamuses live in the wild.

Wild hippopotamuses live only in Africa. They live near lakes or rivers.

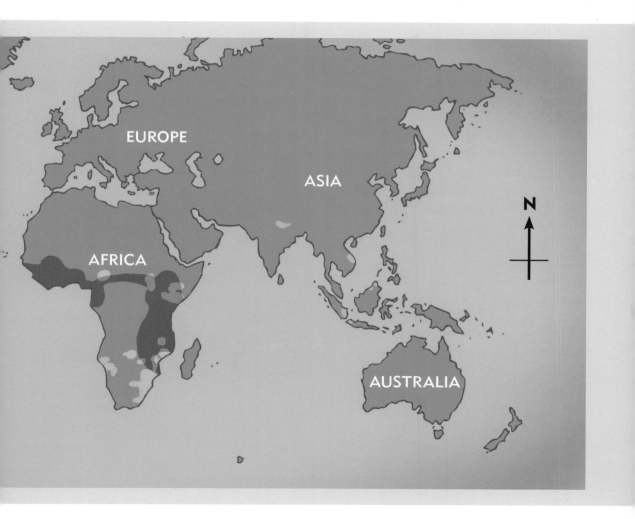

Threats to Survival

The biggest threat to survival for rhinoceroses is **poaching**. Poachers sell rhinoceros horns for use in traditional Chinese medicine.

Wild rhinoceroses are hunted for their horns.

Hippopotamuses are threatened by the clearing of land for farms.

This land has been cleared for farming.

Zoo Homes

In many zoos, rhinoceroses and hippopotamuses live in enclosures. These are often built so they are like the rhinoceroses' and hippopotamuses' homes in the wild.

separate areas for male and female rhinoceroses

dust to roll in

large area to run around in

water to drink

shade

mud to roll in

This enclosure has mud and water, like the rhinoceroses' home in the wild.

Hippopotamuses spend most of their day in the water. They need to soak in large ponds.

shady tree

grassy area to roam on

large pond to soak in

sandy bank to lie on

A hippopotamus enclosure always has plenty of water.

Zoo Food

Rhinoceroses and hippopotamuses need to eat different types of food to stay healthy.

A rhinoceros' zoo food
66 pounds (30 kg) hay
2–3 carrots
2–3 oranges
2–3 apples

A hippopotamus' zoo food
44 pounds (20 kg) hay

A zookeeper prepares hay for the hippopotamuses.

Feeding

Rhinoceroses have two meals of hay each day and a snack of hay at lunchtime. They eat fruit and vegetables as a treat. Hippopotamuses eat several meals of hay each day.

At this zoo, the keeper feeds the rhinoceroses from a truck.

Zoo Health

Zookeepers make sure the rhinoceroses and hippopotamuses are healthy. The keepers check the hippopotamuses' teeth. They check that there are no grass seeds stuck in the hippopotamuses' cheeks.

A zookeeper looks at the hippopotamus' teeth.

Every morning the zookeepers look carefully at the rhinoceroses' skin. They check to make sure there are no cuts or diseases.

A keeper checks the rhinoceros' skin for any injuries or changes.

Baby Rhinoceroses and Hippopotamuses

Rhinoceroses have one baby at a time. The **calves** weigh up to 155 pounds (70 kg) when they are born. They stay with their mother for three years.

A baby rhinoceros stays close to its mother.

Hippopotamuses also have one baby at a time. The calf weighs up to 100 pounds (45 kg) when it is born. The hippopotamus leaves its mother after four years.

Baby hippopotamuses like the water.

How Zoos Are Saving Rhinoceroses and Hippopotamuses

Many kinds of rhinoceros are **endangered**. Some wild rhinoceroses are rescued and taken away from places where they are hunted. They are sent to safe places, such as zoos or national parks.

Many people are needed to capture a wild rhinoceros.

Some zoos donate money to organizations that protect animals in the wild. Save the Rhino and the International Rhino Foundation help save rhinoceroses. They try to prevent poaching.

School students learn about protecting rhinoceroses from zoo notice boards.

Zoos work together by **exchanging** rhinoceroses and hippopotamuses for **breeding**. Pygmy hippopotamuses are very rare in the wild but breed well in zoos. Most pygmy hippopotamuses are now born in zoos.

These rhinoceroses will be moved to other zoos to breed.

Zoos help save rare rhinoceroses, too. The southern white rhinoceros was once very rare. Zoos helped increase their numbers by breeding them. They are now the most common rhinoceroses.

Zoos have helped save the southern white rhinoceros.

Meet Lance, a Hippopotamus Keeper

Lance checks on the hippopotamus.

Question   How did you become a zookeeper?

Answer   I got a job as a tour guide on a **game reserve** in South Africa.

Question   How long have you been a keeper?

Answer   I have worked with animals for five years.

Lance hoses the hippopotamus in its night enclosure.

Question   What animals have you worked with?

Answer   I work with African animals because those are the ones I know best.

Question   What do you like about your job?

Answer   I get to know the animals and they get to know me. I also like working outdoors.

A Day in the Life of a Zookeeper

Zookeepers have certain jobs to do each day. Rhinoceroses are sometimes looked after by a team of zookeepers.

8:00 a.m.

Collect the food for the rhinoceroses and put it on the back of the truck.

9:00 a.m.

Feed the rhinoceroses from the back of the truck.

9:30 a.m.

Check the rhinoceroses' ears and skin to make sure they are healthy.

2:00 p.m.

Check on the young rhinoceroses in the smaller enclosure.

Zoos Around the World

There are many zoos around the world. The Werribee Zoo is near Melbourne, in Australia. The Werribee Zoo keeps nine rhinoceroses in a large, open range area.

Rhinoceroses are fed hay at the Werribee Zoo.

The Werribee Zoo has four female rhinoceroses and five male rhinoceroses. These rhinoceroses have had two calves. The Werribee Zoo plans to breed more rhinoceroses and send them to other zoos.

Southern white rhinoceroses share an enclosure with zebras at the Werribee Zoo.

The Importance of Zoos

Zoos do very important work. They:

- help people learn about animals
- save endangered animals and animals that are treated badly

Southern white rhinoceroses have been saved with the help of zoos.

Glossary

breeding   keeping animals so that they can produce babies

calves   baby rhinoceroses and hippopotamuses

enclosures   the fenced areas where animals are kept in zoos

endangered   at a high risk of becoming extinct

exchanging   swapping

extinct   no longer living on Earth

game reserve   an area of land where wild animals can live safely

poaching   the illegal hunting of animals

wild   living in its natural environment and not taken care of by humans

Index